THE TRUE VINE

*Meditations for a Month
on John 15:1-16*

BY

ANDREW MURRAY

"The mystery which hath been hid
from ages, but now is made manifest to
His saints: to whom God would make
known what is the riches of the glory of
this mystery . . . which is Christ in you,
the hope of glory." COLOSSIANS 1:26-27

MOODY PRESS

CHICAGO

ISBN: 0-8024-8798-X

Printed in the United States of America

1903

ONLY A BRANCH

"I am the vine, ye are the branches." John 15:5

'Tis only a little Branch,
A thing so fragile and weak,
But that little Branch hath a message true
To givo, could it only speak.

"I'm only a little Branch,
I live by a life not mine,
For the sap that flows through my tendrils small
Is the life-blood of the Vine.

"No power indeed have I
The fruit of myself to bear,
But since I'm part of the living Vine,
Its fruitfulness I share.

"Dost thou ask how I abide?
How this life I can maintain? —
I am bound to the Vine by life's strong band,
And I only need remain.

"Where first my life was given,
In the spot where I am set,
Upborne and upheld as the days go by,
By the stem which bears me yet.

"I fear not the days to come,
I dwell not upon the past,
As moment by moment I draw a life,
Which for evermore shall last.

"I bask in the sun's bright beams,
Which with sweetness fills my fruit,
Yet I own not the clusters hanging there,
For they all come from the root."

A life which is not my own,
But another's life in me:
This, this is the message the Branch would speak,
A message to thee and me.

Oh, struggle not to "abide,"
Nor labor to "bring forth fruit,"
But let Jesus unite thee to Himself,
As the Vine Branch to the root.

So simple, so deep, so strong
That union with Him shall be:
His life shall forever replace thine own,
And His love shall flow through thee.

For His Spirit's fruit is love,
And love shall thy life become,
And for evermore on His heart of love
Thy spirit shall have her home.

FREDA HANBURY

4

PREFACE

I HAVE FELT drawn to try to write what young Christians might easily apprehend, as a help to them to take up that position in which the Christian life must be a success. It is as if there is not one of the principal temptations and failures of the Christian life that is not met here. The nearness, the all-sufficiency, the faithfulness of the Lord Jesus, the naturalness, the fruitfulness of a lifo of faith, are so revealed, that it is as if one could with confidence say, Let the parable enter into the heart, and all will be right.

May the blessed Lord give the blessing. May He teach us to study the mystery of the Vine in the spirit of worship, waiting for God's own teaching.

CONTENTS

CONTENTS

THE VINE

I am the True Vine. John 15:1

ALL EARTHLY THINGS are the shadows of heavenly realities—the expression, in created, visible forms, of the invisible glory of God. The Life and the Truth are in Heaven; on earth we have figures and shadows of the heavenly truths. When Jesus says: "I am the true Vine," He tells us that all the vines of earth are pictures and emblems of Himself. He is the divine reality, of which they are the created expression. They all point to Him, and preach Him, and reveal Him. If you would know Jesus, study the vine.

How many eyes have gazed on and admired a great vine with its beautiful fruit. Come and gaze on the heavenly Vine till your eye turns from all else to admire Him. How many, in a sunny clime, sit and rest under the shadow of a vine. Come and be

9

still under the shadow of the true Vine, and rest under it from the heat of the day. What countless numbers rejoice in the fruit of the vine! Come, and take, and eat of the heavenly fruit of the true Vine, and let your soul say: "I sat under His shadow with great delight, and His fruit was sweet to my taste."

I am the true Vine.—This is a heavenly mystery. The earthly vine can teach you much about this Vine of Heaven. Many interesting and beautiful points of comparison suggest themselves, and help us to get conceptions of what Christ meant. But such thoughts do not teach us to know what the heavenly Vine really is, in its cooling shade, and its life-giving fruit. The experience of this is part of the hidden mystery, which none but Jesus Himself, by His Holy Spirit, can unfold and impart.

I am the true Vine.—The vine is the living Lord, who Himself speaks, and gives, and works all that He has for us. If you would know the meaning and power of that word, do not think to find it by thought or study; these may help to show you what you must get from Him to awaken desire and hope and prayer, but they cannot show you the Vine. Jesus alone can reveal Himself. He gives His Holy Spirit to open the eyes to gaze upon Himself, to open the heart to receive Himself. He must Himself speak the word to you and me.

I am the true Vine.—And what am I to do, if I want the mystery, in all its heavenly beauty and blessing, opened up to me? With what you already know of the parable, bow down and be still, worship and wait, until the divine Word enters your heart, and you feel His holy presence with you, and in you. The overshadowing of His holy love will give you the perfect calm and rest of knowing that the Vine will do all.

I am the true Vine.—He who speaks is God, in His infinite power able to enter into us. He is man, one with us. He is the crucified One, who won a perfect righteousness and a divine life for us through His death. He is the glorified One, who from the throne gives His Spirit to make His presence real and true. He speaks—oh, listen, not to His words only, but to Himself, as He whispers secretly day by day: "I am the true Vine! All that the Vine can ever be to its branch, *I will be to you.*"

* * *

Holy Lord Jesus, the heavenly Vine of God's own planting, I beseech Thee, reveal Thyself to my soul. Let the Holy Spirit, not only in thought, but in experience, give me to know all that Thou, the Son of God, art to me as the true Vine.

11

THE HUSBANDMAN

And My Father is the Husbandman. John 15:1

A VINE must have a husbandman to plant and watch over it, to receive and rejoice in its fruit. Jesus says: "My Father is the husbandman." He was "the vine of God's planting." All He was and did, He owed to the Father; in all He only sought the Father's will and glory. He had become man to show us what a creature ought to be to its Creator. He took our place, and the spirit of His life before the Father was ever what He seeks to make ours: "Of him, and through him, and to him are all things." He became the true Vine, that we might be true branches. Both in regard to Christ and ourselves the words teach us the two lessons of absolute dependence and perfect confidence.

My Father is the Husbandman. — Christ

12

ever lived in the spirit of what He once said: "The Son can do nothing of himself." As dependent as a vine is on a husbandman for the place where it is to grow, for its fencing in and watering and pruning, Christ felt Himself entirely dependent on the Father every day for the wisdom and the strength to do the Father's will. As He said in the previous chapter (14:10): "The words that I say unto you, I speak not from Myself; but the Father abiding in Me doeth his works." This absolute dependence had as its blessed counterpart the most blessed confidence that He had nothing to fear: the Father could not disappoint Him. With such a Husbandman as His Father, He could enter death and the grave. He could trust God to raise Him up. All that Christ is and has, He has, not in Himself, but from the Father.

My Father is the Husbandman.—That is as blessedly true for us as for Christ. Christ is about to teach His disciples about their being branches. Before He ever uses the word, or speaks at all of abiding in Him or bearing fruit, He turns their eyes heavenward to the Father watching over them, and working all in them. At the very root of all Christian life lies the thought that God is to do all, that our one work is to give and leave ourselves in His hands, in the confession of utter helplessness and dependence, in the assured confidence that He gives all we need. The great lack of the Christian life is that, even where we trust Christ, we leave God out of the count. Christ came to bring us to God. Christ lived the life of a man exactly as we have to live it. Christ the Vine points to God the Husbandman. As He trusted God, let us trust God, that everything we ought to be and have, as those who belong to the Vine, will be given us from above.

Isaiah said: "A vineyard of red wine; I the Lord do keep it, I will water it every moment; lest any hurt it, I will keep it night and day." Ere we begin to think of fruit or branches, let us have our heart filled with the faith: as glorious as the Vine, is the Husbandman. As high and holy as is our calling, so mighty and loving is the God who will work it all. As surely as the Husbandman made the Vine what it was to be, will He make each branch what it is to be. Our Father is our Husbandman, the Surety for our growth and fruit.

* * *

Blessed Father, we are Thy husbandry. Oh, that Thou mayest have honor of the work of Thy hands! O my Father, I desire to open my heart to the joy of this wondrous truth: My Father is the Husbandman. Teach me to know and trust Thee, and to see that the same deep interest with which Thou caredst for and delightedst in the Vine, extends to every branch, to me too.

THE BRANCH

Every Branch in me That Beareth Not Fruit, He Taketh It Away. John 15:2

HERE WE HAVE one of the chief words of the parable—*branch*. A vine needs branches: without branches it can do nothing, can bear no fruit. As important as it is to know about the Vine, and the Husbandman, it is to realize what the branch is. Before we listen to what Christ has to say about it, let us first of all take in what a branch is, and what it teaches us of our life in Christ. A branch is simply a bit of wood, brought forth by the vine for the one purpose of serving it in bearing its fruit. It is of the very same nature as the vine, and has one life and one spirit with it. Just think a moment of the lessons this suggests.

There is the lesson of *entire consecration*. The branch has but one object for which it exists, one purpose to which it is entirely given up. That is, to bear the fruit the vine wishes to bring forth. And so the believer has but one reason for his being a branch—*but one reason for his existence on earth*—that the heavenly Vine may through him bring forth His fruit. Happy the soul that knows this, that has consented to it, and that says, I have been redeemed and I live for one thing—as exclusively as the natural branch exists only to bring forth fruit, I too; as exclusively as the heavenly Vine exists to bring forth fruit, I too. As I have been planted by God into Christ, I have wholly given myself to bear the fruit the Vine desires to bring forth.

There is the lesson of *perfect conformity*. The branch is exactly like the vine in every aspect—the same nature, the same life, the same place, the same work. In all this they are inseparably one. And so the believer needs to know that he is partaker of the divine nature, and has the very nature and spirit of Christ in him, and that his one calling is to yield himself to a perfect conformity to Christ. The branch is a perfect likeness of the vine; the only difference is, the one is great and strong, and the source of strength, the other little and feeble, ever needing and receiving strength. Even so the believer is, and is to be, the perfect likeness of Christ.

There is the lesson of *absolute dependence.* The vine has its stores of life and sap and strength, not for itself, but for the branches. The branches are and have nothing but what the vine provides and imparts. The believer is called to, and it is his highest blessedness to enter upon, a life of entire and unceasing dependence upon Christ. Day and night, every moment, Christ is to work in him all he needs.

And then the lesson of *undoubting confidence.* The branch has no care; the vine provides all; it has but to yield itself and receive. It is the sight of this truth that leads to the blessed rest of faith, the true secret of growth and strength: "I can do all things through Christ which strengtheneth me."

What a life would come to us if we only consented to be branches! Dear child of God, learn the lesson. You have but one thing to do: Only be a branch—nothing more, nothing less! Just be a branch; Christ will be the Vine that gives all. And the Husbandman, the mighty God, who made the Vine what it is, *will as surely make the branch what it ought to be.*

* * *

Lord Jesus, I pray Thee, reveal to me the heavenly mystery of the branch, in its living union with the Vine, in its claim on all its fulness. And let Thy all-sufficiency, holding and filling Thy branches, lead me to the rest of faith that knows that Thou workest all.

THE FRUIT

Every Branch in me That Beareth Not Fruit, He Taketh It Away. John 15:2

FRUIT.—This is the next great word we have: the Vine, the Husbandman, the branch, the fruit. What has our Lord to say to us of fruit? Simply this—that fruit is the one thing the branch is for, and that if it bear not fruit, the husbandman takes it away. The vine is the glory of the husbandman; the branch is the glory of the vine; the fruit is the glory of the branch; if the branch bring not forth fruit, there is no glory or worth in it; it is an offense and a hindrance; the husbandman takes it away. The one reason for the existence of a branch, the one mark of being a true branch of the heavenly Vine, the one condition of being allowed by the divine Husbandman to share the life of the Vine is—bearing fruit.

And what is fruit? Something that the branch bears, not for itself, but for its owner; something that is to be gathered, and taken away. The branch does indeed receive from the vine sap for its own life, by which it grows thicker and stronger. But this supply for its own maintenance is entirely subordinate to its fulfillment of the purpose of its existence—bearing fruit. It is because Christians do not understand or accept of this truth, that they so fail in their efforts and prayers to live the branch life. They often desire it very earnestly; they read and meditate and pray, and yet they fail, they wonder why? The reason is very simple: they do not know that *fruit-bearing* is the *one thing they have been saved for*. Just as entirely as Christ became the true Vine with the one object, you have been made a branch too, with the one object of bearing fruit for the salvation of men. The Vine and the branch are equally under the unchangeable law of fruit-bearing as the one reason of their being. Christ and the believer, the heavenly Vine and the branch, have equally their place in the world exclusively for one purpose, to carry God's saving love to men. Hence the solemn word: Every branch that beareth not fruit, He taketh it away.

Let us specially beware of one great

mistake. Many Christians think their own salvation is the first thing; their temporal life and prosperity, with the care of their family, the second; and what of time and interest is left may be devoted to fruit-bearing, to the saving of men. No wonder that in most cases very little time or interest can be found. No, Christian, the one object with which you have been made a member of Christ's body is that the Head may have you to carry out His saving work. The one object God had in making you a branch is that Christ may through you bring life to men. Your personal salvation, your business and care for your family, *are entirely subordinate to this.* Your first aim in life, your first aim every day, should be to know how Christ desires to carry out His purpose in you.

Let us begin to think as God thinks. Let us accept Christ's teaching and respond to it. The one object of my being a branch, the one mark of my being a true branch, the one condition of my abiding and growing strong, is that I bear the fruit of the heavenly Vine for dying men to eat and live. And the one thing of which I can have the most perfect assurance is that, with Christ as my Vine, and the Father as my Husband-man, I can indeed be a fruitful branch.

* * *

Our Father, Thou comest seeking fruit. Teach us, we pray Thee, to realize how truly this is the one object of our existence, and of our union to Christ. Make it the one desire of our hearts to be branches, so filled with the Spirit of the Vine, as to bring forth fruit abundantly.

MORE FRUIT

And Every Branch That Beareth Fruit, He Cleanseth, That It May Bear More Fruit.
John 15:2

THE THOUGHT OF FRUIT is so prominent in the eye of Him who sees things as they are, fruit is so truly the one thing God has set His heart upon, that our Lord, after having said that the branch that bears no fruit is taken away, at once adds: and where there is fruit, the one desire of the Husbandman is more fruit. As the gift of His grace, as the token of spiritual vigor, as the showing forth of the glory of God and of Christ, as the only way for satisfying the need of the world, God longs and fits for, more fruit.

More Fruit.—This is a very searching word. As churches and individuals we are in danger of nothing so much as self-contentment. The secret spirit of Laodicea—we are rich and increased in goods, and have need of nothing—may

24

prevail where it is not suspected. The divine warning—poor and wretched and miserable—finds little response just where it is most needed.

Let us not rest content with the thought that we are taking an equal share with others in the work that is being done, or that men are satisfied with our efforts in Christ's service, or even point to us as examples. Let our only desire be to know whether we are bearing all the fruit Christ is willing to give through us as living branches, in close and living union with Himself, whether we are satisfying the loving heart of the great Husbandman, our Father in Heaven, in His desire for more fruit.

More Fruit.—The word comes with divine authority to search and test our life: the true disciple will heartily surrender himself to its holy light, and will earnestly ask that God Himself may show what there may be lacking in the measure or the character of the fruit he bears. Do let us believe that the Word is meant to lead us on to a fuller experience of the Father's purpose of love, of Christ's fullness, and of the wonderful privilege of bearing much fruit in the salvation of men.

More Fruit.—The word is a most encouraging one. Let us listen to it. It is just to the branch that is bearing fruit that the message comes: more fruit. God does not demand this as Pharaoh the taskmaster, or as Moses the lawgiver, without providing the means. He comes as a Father, who gives what He asks, and works what He commands. He comes to us as the living branches of the living Vine, and offers to work the more fruit in us, if we but yield ourselves into His hands. Shall we not admit the claim, accept the offer, and look to Him to work it in us?

"That it may bear more fruit": do let us believe that as the owner of a vine does everything to make the fruitage as rich and large as possible, the divine Husbandman will do all that is needed to make us bear more fruit. All He asks is, that we set our heart's desire on it, entrust ourselves to His working and care, and joyfully look to Him to do His perfect work in us. God has set His heart on more fruit; Christ waits to work it in us; let us joyfully look up to our divine Husbandman and our heavenly Vine, to ensure our bearing more fruit.

* * *

Our Father which art in Heaven, Thou art the heavenly Husbandman. And Christ is the heavenly Vine. And I am a heavenly branch, partaker of His heavenly life, to bear His heavenly fruit. Father, let the power of His life so fill me, that I may ever bear more fruit, to the glory of Thy name.

THE CLEANSING

Every Branch That Beareth Fruit, He Cleanseth It, That It May Bear More Fruit. John 15:2

THERE ARE two remarkable things about the vine. There is not a plant of which the fruit has so much spirit in it, of which spirit can be so abundantly distilled as the vine. And there is not a plant which so soon runs into wild wood, that hinders its fruit, and therefore needs the most merciless pruning. I look out of my window here on large vineyards: the chief care of the vinedresser is the pruning. You may have a trellis vine rooting so deep in good soil that it needs neither digging, nor manuring, nor watering: pruning it cannot dispense with, if it is to bear good fruit. Some trees need occasional pruning; others bear perfect fruit without any: the vine must have it.

And so our Lord tells us, here at the very outset of the parable, that the one work the Father does to the branch that bears fruit is: He cleanseth it, that it may bear more fruit.

Consider a moment what this pruning or cleansing is. It is not the removal of weeds or thorns, or anything from without that may hinder the growth. No; it is the cutting off of the long shoots of the previous year, the removal of something that comes from within, that has been produced by the life of the vine itself. It is the removal of something that is a proof of the vigor of its life; the more vigorous the growth has been, the greater the need for the pruning. It is the honest, healthy wood of the vine that has to be cut away. And why? Because it would consume too much of the sap to fill all the long shoots of last year's growth: the sap must be saved up and used for fruit alone. The branches, sometimes eight and ten feet long, are cut down close to the stem, and nothing is left but just one or two inches of wood, enough to bear the grapes. It is when everything that is not needful for fruit-bearing has been relentlessly cut down, and just as little of the branches as possible has been left, that full, rich fruit may be expected.

What a solemn, precious lesson! It is not

to sin only that the cleansing of the Husbandman here refers. It is to our own religious activity, as it is developed in the very act of bearing fruit. It is this that must be cut down and cleansed away. We have, in working for God, to use our natural gifts of wisdom, or eloquence, or influence, or zeal. And yet they are ever in danger of being unduly developed, and then trusted in. And so, after each season of work, God has to bring us to the end of ourselves, to the consciousness of the helplessness and the danger of all that is of man, to feel that we are nothing. All that is to be left of us is just enough to receive the power of the life-giving sap of the Holy Spirit. What is of man must be reduced to its very lowest measure. All that is inconsistent with the most entire devotion to Christ's service must be removed. The more perfect the cleansing and cutting away of all that is of self, the less of surface over which the Holy Spirit is to be spread, so much the more intense can be the concentration of our whole being, to be entirely at the disposal of the Spirit. This is the true circumcision of the heart, the circumcision of Christ. This is the true crucifixion with Christ, bearing about the dying of the Lord Jesus in the body.

Blessed cleansing, God's own cleansing!

How we may rejoice in the assurance that we shall bring forth more fruit.

* * *

O our holy Husbandman, cleanse and cut away all that there is in us that would make a fair show, or could become a source of self-confidence and glorying. Lord, keep us very low, that no flesh may glory in Thy presence. We do trust Thee to do Thy work.

THE PRUNING KNIFE

Already Ye Are Clean Because of The Word I Have Spoken Unto You. John 15:3

WHAT IS THE PRUNING KNIFE of this heavenly Husbandman? It is often said to be affliction, but is this the tool He uses? How would it then fare with many who have long seasons free from adversity; or with some on whom God appears to shower down kindness all their life long? No; it is the Word of God that is the knife, sharper than any two-edged sword, that pierces even to the dividing asunder of the soul and spirit, and is quick to discern the thoughts and intents of the heart. It is only when affliction leads to this discipline of the Word that it becomes a blessing; the lack of this heart-cleansing through the Word is the reason why affliction is so often unsanctified. Not even Paul's thorn in the flesh could become a blessing until Christ's Word—"My strength is made perfect in weakness"—had made him see the danger of self-exaltation, and made him willing to rejoice in infirmities.

The Word is God's pruning knife. Jesus says: "Ye are already clean, because of the word I have spoken unto you." How searchingly that word had been spoken by Him, out of whose mouth there went a sharp two-edged sword, as He had taught them! "Except a man deny himself, lose his life, forsake all, hate father and mother, he cannot be My disciple, he is not worthy of Me"; or as He humbled their pride, or reproved their lack of love, or foretold their all forsaking Him. From the opening of His ministry in the Sermon on the Mount to His words of warning in the last night, His Word had tried and cleansed them. He had discovered and condemned all there was of self; they were now emptied and cleansed, ready for the incoming of the Holy Spirit.

It is as the soul gives up its own thoughts, and men's thoughts of what is religion, and yields itself heartily, humbly, patiently, to the teaching of the Word by the Spirit, that the Father will do His blessed work of pruning and cleansing away all of nature and self that mixes with our work and hinders His Spirit. Let those who would know

all the Husbandman can do for them, all
the Vine can bring forth through them, seek
earnestly to yield themselves heartily to the
blessed cleansing through the Word. Let
them, in their study of the Word, receive it
as a hammer that breaks and opens up, as
a fire that melts and refines, as a sword
that lays bare and slays all that is of the
flesh. The word of conviction will prepare
for the word of comfort and of hope, and
the Father will cleanse them through the
Word.

All ye who are branches of the true Vine,
each time you read or hear the Word, wait
first of all on Him to use it for His cleansing
of the branch. Set your heart upon His
desire for more fruit. Trust Him as Husbandman to work it. Yield yourselves in
simple childlike surrender to the cleansing
work of His Word and Spirit, and you may
count upon it that His purpose will be
fulfilled in you.

* * *

Father, I pray Thee, cleanse me through Thy
Word. Let it search out and bring to light all
that is of self and the flesh in my religion. Let it
cut away every root of self-confidence, that the
Vine may find me wholly free to receive His life
and Spirit. O my holy Husbandman, I trust
Thee to care for the branch as much as for the
Vine. Thou only art my hope.

ABIDE

Abide In Me, And I In You. John 15:4

WHEN A NEW GRAFT is placed in a vine, and it abides there, there is a twofold process that takes place. The first is in the wood. The graft shoots its little roots and fibers down into the stem, and the stem grows up into the graft, and what has been called the structural union is effected. The graft abides and becomes one with the vine, and even though the vine were to die, would still be one wood with it. Then there is the second process, in which the sap of the vine enters the new structure, and uses it as a passage through which sap can flow up to show itself in young shoots and leaves and fruit. Here is the vital union. Into the graft which abides in the stock, the stock enters with sap to abide in it.

When our Lord says: "Abide in me, and I in you," He points to something analogous to this. "Abide in me": that refers more to that which we have to do. We have to trust and obey, to detach ourselves from all else, to reach out after Him and cling to Him, to sink ourselves into Him. As we do this, through the grace He gives, a character is formed, and a heart prepared for the fuller experience: "I in you." God strengthens us with might by the Spirit in the inner man, and Christ dwells in the heart by faith.

Many believers pray and long very earnestly for the filling of the Spirit and the indwelling of Christ, and wonder that they do not make more progress. The reason is often this, the "I in you" cannot come because the "abide in me" is not maintained. "There is one body and one spirit"; before the Spirit can fill, there must be a body prepared. The graft must have grown into the stem, and be abiding in it before the sap can flow through to bring forth fruit. It is as in lowly obedience we follow Christ, even in external things, denying ourselves, forsaking the world, and even in the body seeking to be conformable to Him, as we thus seek to abide in Him, that we shall be able to receive and enjoy the "I in you." The work enjoined on us: *"Abide in*

35

me," will prepare us for the work undertaken by Him: *"I in you."*

In. —The two parts of the injunction have their unity in that central deep-meaning word *in*. There is no deeper word in Scripture. God is *in all.* God dwells *in* Christ. Christ lives *in* God. We are *in* Christ. Christ is *in* us: our life taken up into His; His life received into ours; in a divine reality that words cannot express, we are *in* Him and He *in* us. And the words, "Abide in me and I in you," just tell us to believe in this divine mystery, and to count upon our God the Husbandman, and Christ the Vine, to make it divinely true. No thinking or teaching or praying can grasp it; it is a divine mystery of love. As little as we can effect the union can we understand it. Let us just look upon this infinite, divine, omnipotent Vine loving us, holding us, working in us. Let us in the faith of His working abide and rest in Him, ever turning heart and hope to Him alone. And let us count upon Him to fulfill in us the mystery: "Ye in me, and I in you."

* * *

Blessed Lord, Thou dost bid me abide in Thee. How can I, Lord, except Thou show Thyself to me, waiting to receive and welcome and keep me? I pray Thee show me how Thou as Vine undertaketh to do all. To be occupied

36

with Thee is to abide in Thee. Here I am, Lord, a branch, cleansed and abiding—resting in Thee, and awaiting the inflow of Thy life and grace.

EXCEPT YE ABIDE

As The Branch Cannot Bear Fruit Of Itself, Except It Abide In The Vine; No More Can Ye, Except Ye Abide In Me. John 15:4

WE KNOW THE MEANING of the word *except*. It expresses some indispensable condition, some inevitable law. "The branch cannot bear fruit of itself, *except* it abide in the vine. No more can ye, except ye abide in me." There is but one way for the branch to bear fruit, there is no other possibility, it must abide in unbroken communion with the vine. Not of itself, but only of the vine, does the fruit come. Christ had already said: "Abide in me"; in nature the branch teaches us the lesson so clearly; it is such a wonderful privilege to be called and allowed to abide in the heavenly Vine; one might have thought it needless to add these words of warning. But no—Christ knows so well what a renunciation of self is implied in this: "Abide in me"; how strong and universal the tendency would be to seek to bear fruit by our own efforts; how difficult it would be to get us to believe that actual, continuous abiding in Him is an absolute necessity! He insists upon the truth: *Not of itself* can the branch bear fruit; *except it abide,* it cannot bear fruit. "No more can ye, *except ye abide in me."*

But must this be taken literally? Must I, as exclusively, and manifestly, and unceasingly, and absolutely, as the branch abides in the vine, be equally given up to find my whole life in Christ alone? I must indeed. The *except ye abide* is as universal as the except it abide. The *no more can ye* admits of no exception or modification. If I am to be a true branch, if I am to bear fruit, if I am to be what Christ as Vine wants me to be, my whole existence must be as exclusively devoted to abiding in Him, as that of the natural branch is to abiding in its vine.

Let me learn the lesson. Abiding is to be an act of the will and the whole heart. Just as there are degrees in seeking and serving God, "not with a perfect heart," or "with the whole heart," so there may be degrees in abiding. In regeneration the divine life enters us, but does not all at once master and fill our whole being. This comes as matter of command and obedience. There is unspeakable danger of our not giving ourselves with our whole heart to abide. There is unspeakable danger of our giving ourselves to work for God, and to bear fruit, with but little of the true abiding, the wholehearted losing of ourselves in Christ and His life. There is unspeakable danger of much work with but little fruit, for lack of this vital relationship. We must allow the words, "not of itself," "except it abide," to do their work of searching and exposing, of pruning and cleansing, all that there is of self-will and self-confidence in our life; this will deliver us from this great evil, and so prepare us for His teaching, giving the full meaning of the word in us: "Abide in me, and I in you."

Our blessed Lord desires to call us away from ourselves and our own strength, to Himself and His strength. Let us accept the warning, and turn with great fear and self-distrust to Him to do His work. "Our life is hid with Christ in God!" That life is a heavenly mystery, hid from the wise even among Christians, and revealed unto babes. The childlike spirit learns that life is given from Heaven every day and every moment to the soul that accepts the teaching: "not of itself," "except it abide," and seeks its all in the Vine. Abiding in the Vine then comes to be nothing more nor less than the restful surrender of the soul to let Christ have all and work all, as completely as in nature the branch knows and seeks nothing but the vine.

*   *   *

Abide in Me. I have heard, my Lord, that with every command, Thou also givest the power to obey. With Thy "rise and walk," the lame man leaped. I accept Thy word, *"Abide in me,"* as a word of power, that gives power, and even now I say, Yea, Lord, I will, I do abide in Thee.

I THE VINE

I Am The Vine, Ye Are The Branches.
John 15:5

IN THE PREVIOUS VERSE Christ has just said: "Abide in me," He then announced the great unalterable law of all branch-life, on earth or in Heaven: *"not of itself"; "except it abide."* In the opening words of the parable He has already spoken: "I am the vine." He now repeats the words. He would have as understand—note well the lesson, simple as it appears, it is the key of the abiding life—that the only way to obey the command, "Abide in me," is to have eye and heart fixed upon Himself. "Abide in me . . . I am the true vine." Yes, study this holy mystery until you see Christ as the true Vine, bearing, strengthening, supplying, inspiring all His branches, *being and doing in each branch all it needs,* and

42

the abiding will come of itself. Yes, gaze upon Him as the true Vine, until you feel what a heavenly Mystery it is, and are compelled to ask the Father to reveal it to you by His Holy Spirit. He to whom God reveals the glory of the true Vine, he who sees what Jesus is and waits to do every moment, he cannot but abide. The vision of Christ is an irresistible attraction; it draws and holds us like a magnet. Listen ever to the living Christ still speaking to you, and waiting to show you the meaning and power of His Word: *"I am the vine."*

How much weary labor there has been in striving to understand what abiding is, how much fruitless effort in trying to attain it! Why was this? Because the attention was turned to the abiding as a work we have to do, instead of the living Christ, in whom we were to be kept abiding, who Himself was to hold and keep us. We thought of abiding as a continual strain and effort—we forget that it means rest from effort to one who has found the place of his abode. Do notice how Christ said, "Abide *in Me;* I am the Vine that brings forth, and holds, and strengthens, and makes fruitful the branches. Abide in Me, rest in Me, and let Me do My work. I am the true Vine, all I am, and speak, and do is divine truth, giving the actual reality of what is said. I am the

Vine, only consent and yield thy all to Me, I will do all in thee."

And so it sometimes comes that souls who have never been specially occupied with the thought of abiding, are abiding all the time, because they are occupied with Christ. Not that the word *abide* is not needful; Christ used it so often, because it is the very key to the Christian life. But He would have us understand it in its true sense —"Come out of every other place, and every other trust and occupation, come out of self with its reasonings and efforts, come and rest in what I shall do. Live out of thyself; abide *in Me*. Know that thou art *in Me*; thou needest no more; remain there *in Me*."

"I am the vine." Christ did not keep this mystery hidden from His disciples. He revealed it, first in words here, then in power when the Holy Spirit came down. He will reveal it to us too, first in the thoughts and confessions and desires these words awaken, then in power by the Spirit. Do let us wait on Him to show us all the heavenly meaning of the mystery. Let each day, in our quiet time, in the inner chamber with Him and His Word, our chief thought and aim be to get the heart fixed on Him, in the assurance: all that a vine ever can do for its branches, my Lord Jesus will do, is doing, for me. Give Him time, give Him your ear, that He may whisper and explain the divine secret: "I am the vine."

Above all, remember, Christ is the Vine of God's planting, and you are a branch of God's grafting. Stand always before God, in Christ,—waiting for all grace from God, in Christ, yielding yourself to bear the more fruit the Husbandman asks, in Christ. And pray much for the revelation of the mystery that all the love and power of God that rested on Christ is working in you too. "I am God's Vine," Jesus says; "all I am I have from Him; all I am is for you; God will work it in you."

* * *

I am the Vine. Blessed Lord, speak Thou that word into my soul. Then shall I know that all Thy fullness is for me. And that I can count upon Thee to stream it into me, and that my abiding is so easy and so sure when I forget and lose myself in the adoring faith that the Vine holds the branch and supplies its every need.

YE THE BRANCHES

I Am The Vine, Ye Are The Branches.
John 15:5

CHRIST HAS ALREADY said much of the branch; here He comes to the personal application: "Ye are the branches of whom I have been speaking. As I am the Vine, engaged to be and do all the branches need, so I now ask you, in the new dispensation of the Holy Spirit whom I have been promising you, to accept the place I give you, and to be My branches on earth." The relationship He seeks to establish is an intensely personal one: it all hinges on the two little words *I* and *You*. And it is for us as intensely personal as for the first disciples. Let us present ourselves before our Lord, until He speaks to each of us in power, and our whole soul feels it: "I am the Vine; you are the branch."

Dear disciple of Jesus, however young or feeble, hear the voice, "You are the branch." You must be *nothing less*. Let no false humility, no carnal fear of sacrifice, no unbelieving doubts as to what you feel able for, keep you back from saying: "I will be a branch, with all that may mean—a branch, very feeble, but yet as like the Vine as can be, for I am of the same nature, and receive of the same spirit. A branch, utterly helpless, and yet just as manifestly set apart before God and men, as wholly given up to the work of bearing fruit, as the Vine itself. A branch, nothing in myself, and yet resting and rejoicing in the faith that knows that He will provide for all. Yes, by His grace, I will be nothing less than a branch, and all He means it to be, that through me, He may bring forth His fruit."

You are the branch.—You need be *nothing more.* You need not for one single moment of the day take upon you the responsibility of the Vine. You need not leave the place of entire dependence and unbounded confidence. You need, least of all, to be anxious as to how you are to understand the mystery, or fulfill its conditions, or work out its blessed aim. The Vine will give all and work all. The Father, the Husbandman, watches over your union with and growth in the Vine. You need be nothing more than a branch. Only a branch! Let that be your watchword; it will lead in the path of continual surrender to Christ's working, of true obedience to His every command, of joyful expectancy of all His grace.

Is there anyone who now asks: "How can I learn to say this aright, 'Only a branch!' and to live it out?" Dear soul, the character of a branch, its strength, and the fruit it bears, depend entirely upon the Vine. And your life as branch depends entirely upon your apprehension of what our Lord Jesus is. Therefore never separate the two words: "I the Vine—you the branch." Your life and strength and fruit depend upon what your Lord Jesus is! Therefore worship and trust Him; let Him be your one desire and the one occupation of your heart. And when you feel that you do not and cannot know Him aright, then just remember it is part of His responsibility as Vine to make Himself known to you. He does this not in thoughts and conceptions—no—but in a hidden growth within the life that is humbly and restfully and entirely given up to wait on Him. The Vine reveals itself within the branch; thence comes the growth and fruit, Christ dwells and works within His branch; only be a branch, waiting on Him to do all; He will be to thee the true Vine. The Father Himself, the divine Husbandman, is able to make you a branch worthy of the heavenly Vine. You shall not be disappointed.

* * *

Ye are the branches. This word, too Lord!-O speak it in power unto my soul. Let not the branch of the earthly vine put me to shame, but as it only lives to bear the fruit of the vine, may my life on earth have no wish or aim, but to let Thee bring forth fruit through me.

MUCH FRUIT

He That Abideth in Me, and I in Him, the Same Bringeth Forth Much Fruit. John 15:5

OUR LORD has spoken of fruit, more fruit. He now adds the thought: much fruit. There is in the Vine such fullness, the care of the divine Husbandman is so sure of success, that the much fruit is not a demand, but the simple promise of what must come to the branch that lives in the double abiding—he in Christ, and Christ in him. "The same bringeth forth much fruit." It is certain.

Have you ever noticed the difference in the Christian life between work and fruit? A machine can do work: only life can bear fruit. A law can compel work: only love can spontaneously bring forth fruit. Work implies effort and labor: the essential idea of fruit is that it is the silent natural restful produce of our inner life. The gardener

50

may labor to give his apple tree the digging and manuring, the watering and the pruning it needs; he can do nothing to produce the apple: the tree bears its own fruit. So in the Christian life: "The fruit of the Spirit is love, peace, joy." The healthy life bears much fruit. The connection between work and fruit is perhaps best seen in the expression, "fruitful in every good work" (Col. 1:10). It is only when good works come as the fruit of the indwelling Spirit that they are acceptable to God. Under the compulsion of law and conscience, or the influence of inclination and zeal, men may be most diligent in good works, and yet find that they have but little spiritual result. There can be no reason but this—their works are man's effort, instead of being the fruit of the Spirit, the restful, natural outcome—of the Spirit's operation within us.

Let all workers come and listen to our holy Vine as He reveals the law of sure and abundant fruitfulness: "He that abideth in me, and I in him, the same bringeth forth much fruit." The gardener cares for one thing—the strength and healthy life of his tree: the fruit follows of itself. If you would bear fruit, see that the inner life is perfectly right, that your relation to Christ Jesus is clear and close. Begin each day with Him in the morning, to know in truth that you are abiding in Him and He in you. Christ tells that nothing less will do. It is not your willing and running, it is not by your might or strength, but—"by my Spirit, saith the Lord." Meet each new engagement, undertake every new work, with an ear and heart open to the Master's voice: "He that abideth in me, beareth much fruit." You see to the abiding; He will see to the fruit, for He will give it in you and through you.

O my brother, it is Christ who must do all! The Vine provides the sap, and the life, and the strength: the branch waits, and rests, and receives, and bears the fruit. Oh, the blessedness of being only branches, through whom the Spirit flows and brings God's life to men!

I pray you, take time and ask the Holy Spirit to help you to realize the unspeakably solemn place you occupy in the mind of God. He has planted you into His Son with the calling and the power to bear *much fruit*. Accept that place. Look always to God, and to Christ, and expect joyfully to be what God has planned to make you, a fruitful branch.

* * *

Much fruit! So be it, blessed Lord Jesus. It can be, for Thou are the Vine. It shall be, for I am abiding in Thee. It must be, for Thy Father is the Husbandman that cleanses the branch. Yes, much fruit, out of the abundance of Thy grace.

YOU CAN DO NOTHING

Apart From Me Ye Can Do Nothing. John 15:5

IN EVERYTHING the life of the branch is to be the exact counterpart of that of the Vine. Of Himself Jesus had said: "The Son can do nothing of himself." As the outcome of that entire dependence, He could add: "All that the Father doeth, doeth the Son also likewise." As Son He did not receive His life from the Father once for all, but moment by moment. His life was a continual waiting on the Father for all He was to do. And so Christ says of His disciples: "Ye can do nothing apart from me." He means it literally. To everyone who wants to live the true disciple life, to bring forth fruit and glorify God, the message comes: You can do nothing. What has been said: "He that abideth in me, and I in him, the

54

same beareth much fruit," is here enforced by the simplest and strongest of arguments: "Abiding in Me is indispensable, for, you know it, of yourselves you can do nothing to maintain or act out the heavenly life."

A deep conviction of the truth of this word lies at the very root of a strong spiritual life. As little as I created myself, as little as I could raise a man from the dead, can I give myself the divine life. As little as I can give it myself, can I maintain or increase it: every motion is the work of God through Christ and His Spirit. It is as a man believes this, that he will take up that position of entire and continual dependence which is the very essence of the life of faith. With the spiritual eye he sees Christ every moment supplying grace for every breathing and every deepening of the spiritual life. His whole heart says Amen to the word: You can do nothing. And just because he does so, he can also say: "I can do all things in Christ who strengtheneth me." The sense of helplessness, and the abiding to which it compels, leads to true fruitfulness and diligence in good works.

Apart from me ye can do nothing—what a plea and what a call every moment to abide in Christ! We have only to go back to the vine to see how true it is. Look again at that little branch, utterly helpless and fruitless except as it receives sap from the vine, and learn that the full conviction of not being able to do anything apart from Christ is just what you need to teach you to abide in your heavenly Vine. It is this that is the great meaning of the pruning Christ spoke of—all that is self must be brought low, that our confidence may be in Christ alone. "Abide in me"—much fruit! "Apart from me"—nothing! Ought there to be any doubt as to what we shall choose?

The one lesson of the parable is—as surely, as naturally as the branch abides in the vine, *You can abide in Christ.* For this He is the true Vine; for this God is the Husbandman; for this you are a branch. Shall we not cry to God to deliver us forever from the "apart from me," and to make the "abide in me" an unceasing reality? Let your heart go out to what Christ is, and can do, to His divine power and His tender love to each of His branches, and you will say with increasing confidence: "Lord! I am abiding; I will bear much fruit. My impotence is my strength. So be it. Apart from Thee, nothing. In Thee, much fruit."

* * *

Apart from Me—you nothing. Lord, I gladly accept the arrangement: I nothing—Thou all.

My nothingness is my highest blessing, because Thou art the Vine, that givest and workest all. So be it, Lord! I, nothing, ever waiting on Thy fullness. Lord, reveal to me the glory of this blessed life.

WITHERED BRANCHES

If a Man Abide Not in Me, He is Cast Forth as a Branch, and is Withered; and They Gather Them, and Cast Them into the Fire, and They are Burned: John 15:6

THE LESSONS these words teach are very simple and very solemn. A man can come to such a connection with Christ, that he counts himself to be in Him, and yet he can be cast forth. There is such a thing as not abiding in Christ, which leads to withering up and burning. There is such a thing as a withered branch, one in whom the initial union with Christ appears to have taken place, and in whom yet it is seen that his faith was but for a time. What a solemn call to look around and see if there be not withered branches in our churches, to look within and see whether we are indeed abiding and bearing fruit!

And what may be the cause of this "not abiding"? With some it is that they never understood how the Christian calling leads to holy obedience and to loving service. They were content with the thought that they had believed, and were safe from Hell; there was neither motive nor power to abide in Christ—they knew not the need of it. With others it was that the cares of the world, or its prosperity, choked the Word: they had never forsaken all to follow Christ. With still others it was that their religion and their faith was in the wisdom of men, and not in the power of God. They trusted in the means of grace, or in their own sincerity, or in the soundness of their faith in justifying grace; they had never come even to seek an entire abiding in Christ as their only safety. No wonder that, when the hot winds of temptation or persecution blew, they withered away: they were not truly rooted in Christ.

Let us open our eyes and see if there be not withered branches all around us in the churches. Young men, whose confessions were once bright, but who are growing cold. Or old men, who have retained their profession, but out of whom the measure of life there once appeared to be has died out. Let ministers and believers take Christ's words to heart, and see, and ask the Lord whether there is nothing to be done for branches that are beginning to wither. And let the word *Abide* ring through the Church until every believer has caught it—no safety but in a true abiding in Christ.

Let each of us turn within. Is our life fresh, and green, and vigorous, bringing forth its fruit in its season? (See Ps. 1:3; 92:13, 14: Jer. 17:7, 8.) Let us accept every warning with a willing mind, and let Christ's "if a man abide not" give new urgency to His "abide in me." To the upright soul the secret of abiding will become ever simpler, just the consciousness of the place in which He has put me; just the childlike resting in my union with Him, and the trustful assurance that He will keep me. Oh, do let us believe there is a life that knows of no withering, that is ever green; and that brings forth fruit abundantly!

* * *

Withered! O my Father, watch over me, and keep me, and let nothing ever for a moment hinder the freshness that comes from a full abiding in the Vine. Let the very thought of a withered branch fill me with holy fear and watchfulness.

WHATSOEVER YE WILL

If Ye Abide in Me, and My Words Abide in You, Ask Whatsoever Ye Will, and it Shall be Done Unto You. John 15:7

THE WHOLE PLACE of the branch in the vine is one of unceasing prayer. Without intermission it is ever calling: "O my vine, send the sap I need to bear Thy fruit." And its prayers are never unanswered: it asks what it needs, what it will, and it is done.

The healthy life of the believer in Christ is equally one of unceasing prayer. Consciously or unconsciously, he lives in continual dependence. The Word of his Lord, "You can do nothing," has taught him that not more unbroken than the continuance of the branch in the vine, must be his asking and receiving. The promise of our text gives us infinite boldness: "Ask whatsoever ye will, and it shall be done unto you."

61

The promise is given in direct connection with fruit-bearing. Limit it to yourself and your own needs, and you rob it of its power; you rob yourself of the power of appropriating it. Christ was sending these disciples out, and they were ready to give their life for the world; to them He gave the disposal of the treasures of Heaven. Their prayers would bring the Spirit and the power they needed for their work.

The promise is given in direct connection with the coming of the Spirit. The Spirit is not mentioned in the parable, just as little as the sap of the vine is mentioned. But both are meant all through. In the chapter preceding the parable, our Lord had spoken of the Holy Spirit, in connection with their inner life, being in them, and revealing Himself within them (14:15-23). In the next chapter He speaks of the Holy Spirit in connection with their work, coming to them, convincing the world, and glorifying Him (16:7-14). To avail ourselves of the unlimited prayer promises, we must be men who are filled with the Spirit, and wholly given up to the work and glory of Jesus. The Spirit will lead us into the truth of its meaning and the certainty of its fulfillment.

Let us realize that we can only fulfill our calling to bear much fruit, by praying

much. In Christ are hid all the treasures
men around us need; in Him all God's
children are blessed with all spiritual
blessings; He is full of grace and truth. But
it needs prayer, much prayer, strong
believing prayer, to bring these blessings
down. And let us equally remember that
we cannot appropriate the promise without
a life given up for men. Many try to take the
promise, and then look round for what they
can ask. This is not the way; but the very
opposite. Get the heart burdened with the
need of souls, and the command to save
them, and the power will come to claim the
promise.

Let us claim it as one of the revelations
of our wonderful life in the Vine: He tells us
that if we ask in His name, in virtue of our
union with Him, whatsoever it be, it will be
done to us. Souls are perishing because
there is too little prayer. God's children are
feeble because there is too little prayer.
We bear so little fruit because there is so
little prayer. The faith of this promise
would make us strong to pray; let us not
rest till it has entered into our very heart,
and drawn us in the power of Christ to con-
tinue and labor and strive in prayer until
the blessing comes in power. To be a
branch means not only bearing fruit on
earth, but power in prayer to bring down

63

blessing from Heaven. Abiding fully means praying much.

* * *

Ask what ye will. O my Lord, why is it that our hearts are so little able to accept these words in their divine simplicity? Oh, help me to see what we need nothing less than this promise to overcome the powers of the world and Satan! Teach us to pray in the faith of this Thy promise.

IF YE ABIDE

If Ye Abide in Me, and My Words Abide in You, Ask Whatsoever Ye Will, and it Shall be Done Unto You. John 15:7

THE REASON the Vine and its branches are such a true parable of the Christian life is that all nature has one source and breathes one spirit. The plant world was created to be to man an object lesson teaching him his entire dependence upon God, and his security in that dependence. He that clothes the lilies will much more clothe us. He that gives the trees and the vines their beauty and their fruits, making each what He meant it to be, will much more certainly make us what He would have us to be. The only difference is, what God works in the trees is by a power of which they are not conscious. He wants to work in us with our consent. This is the nobility of man, that he has a will that can co-operate with God in understanding and approving and accepting what He offers to do.

If ye abide.—Here is the difference between the branch of the natural and the branch of the spiritual Vine. The former abides by force of nature: the latter abides, not by force of will, but by a divine power given to the consent of the will. Such is the wonderful provision God has made that, what the power of nature does in the one case, the power of grace will do in the other. The branch can abide in the Vine.

If ye abide in me . . . ask whatsoever ye will.—If we are to live a true prayer life, with the love and the power and the experience of prayer marking it, there must be no question about the abiding. And if we abide, there need be no question about the liberty of asking what we will, and the certainty of its being done. There is the one condition: "If ye abide in me." There must be no hesitation about the possibility or the certainty of it. We must gaze on that little branch and its wonderful power of bearing such beautiful fruit until we truly learn to abide.

And what is its secret? Be wholly occupied with Jesus. Sink the roots of your being in faith and love and obedience deep down into Him. Come away out of every other place to abide here. Give up everything for the inconceivable privilege of being a branch on earth of the glorified Son of God in Heaven. Let Christ be first. Let Christ be all. Do not be occupied with the abiding—be occupied with Christ. He will hold you, He will keep you abiding in Him. He will abide in you.

If ye abide in me, and my words abide in you.—This He gives as the equivalent of the other expression: "I in you. If my words abide in You"—that is, not only in meditation, in memory, in love, in faith—all these are needed—but above all, in obedience. If these words enter into your will, your being, and constitute your life—if they transform your character into their own likeness, and you become and are what they speak and mean—ask what ye will; it shall be done unto you. Your words to God in prayer will be the fruit of Christ and His words living in you.

Ask what ye will, and it shall be done unto you.—Believe in the truth of this promise. Set yourself to be an intercessor for men; a fruit-bearing intercessor, always calling down more blessing. Such faith and prayer will help you wonderfully to abide wholly and unceasingly.

* * *

If ye abide. Yes, Lord, the power to pray and the power to prevail must depend on this abiding in Thee. As Thou art the Vine, Thou art the divine Intercessor, who breathest Thy spirit in us. Oh, for grace to abide simply and wholly in Thee, and ask great things!

THE FATHER GLORIFIED

Herein is My Father Glorified, that Ye Bear Much Fruit. John 15:8

How can we glorify God? Not by adding to His glory or bringing Him any new glory that He has not. But simply by allowing His glory to shine out through us, by yielding ourselves to Him, that His glory may manifest itself in us and through us to the world. In a vineyard or a vine bearing much fruit, the owner is glorified, as it tells of his skill and care. In the disciple who bears much fruit, the Father is glorified. Before men and angels, proof is given of the glory of God's grace and power; God's glory shines out through him.

This is what Peter means when he writes: "He that ministers, let him minister as of the ability that God giveth, that God in all things may be glorified through Jesus Christ." As a man works and serves in a power which comes from God alone, God gets all the glory. When we confess that the ability came from God alone, he that does the work, and they who see it, equally glorify God. It was God who did it. Men judge by the fruit of a garden the worth of the gardener. Men judge God by the fruit that the branches of the Vine of His planting bears. Little fruit brings little glory to God. It brings no honor to either the Vine or the Husbandman. "That ye bear much fruit, herein is my Father glorified."

We have sometimes mourned our lack of fruit, as a loss to ourselves and our fellow men, with complaints of our feebleness as the cause. Let us rather think of the sin and shame of little fruit as robbing God of the glory He ought to get from us. Let us learn the secret of bringing glory to God, serving of the ability which God giveth. The full acceptance of Christ's Word, "You can do nothing"; the simple faith in God, who worketh all in all; the abiding in Christ through whom the divine Husbandman does His work and gets much fruit—this is the life that will bring glory to God.

Much fruit.—God asks it; see that you give it. God can be content with nothing less; you be content with nothing less. Let these words of Christ—fruit, more fruit, much fruit—abide in you, until you think as He does, and you be prepared to take from Him, the heavenly Vine, what He has for you. Much fruit: herein is my Father glorified. Let the very height of the demand be your encouragement. It is so entirely beyond your power, that it throws you more entirely upon Christ, your true Vine. He can, He will, make it true in you.

Much fruit.—God asks because He needs. He does not ask fruit from the branches of His Vine for show, to prove what He can do. No; He needs it for the salvation of men: it is in that He is to be glorified. Throw yourself in much prayer on your Vine and your Husbandman. Cry to God and your Father to give you fruit to bring to men. Take the burden of the hungry and the perishing on you, as Jesus did when He was moved with compassion, and your power in prayer, and your abiding, and your bearing much fruit to the glory of the Father will have a reality and a certainty you never knew before.

* * *

The Father glorified. Blessed prospect—God glorifying Himself in me, showing forth the glory of His goodness and power in what He works in me, and through me. What a motive to bear much fruit, just as much as He works in me! Father, glorify Thyself in me.

TRUE DISCIPLES

---

*Herein is My Father Glorified, that Ye Bear
Much Fruit: So Shall Ye Be My Disciples.*
John 15:8

AND ARE THOSE who do not bear much fruit
not disciples? They may be, but in a back-
ward and immature stage. Of those who
bear much fruit, Christ says: "These are
My disciples, such as I would have them
be—these are true disciples." Just as we
say of someone in whom the idea of
manliness is realized: That is a man! So our
Lord tells who are disciples after His
heart, worthy of the name: Those who bear
much fruit. We find this double sense of the
word *disciple* in the Gospel. Sometimes it is
applied to all who accepted Christ's
teaching. At other times it includes only the
inner circle of those who followed Christ
wholly, and gave themselves to His training

for service. The difference has existed throughout all ages. There have always been a smaller number of God's people who have sought to serve Him with their whole heart, while the majority have been content with a very small measure of the knowledge of His grace and will.

And what is the difference between this smaller inner circle and the many who do not seek admission to it? We find it in the words: *much fruit*. With many Christians the thought of personal safety, which at their first awakening was a legitimate one, remains to the end the one aim of their religion. The idea of service and fruit is always a secondary and very subordinate one. The honest longing for much fruit does not trouble them. Souls that have heard the call to live wholly for their Lord, to give their life for Him as He gave His for them, can never be satisfied with this. Their cry is to bear as much fruit as they possibly can, as much as their Lord ever can desire or give in them.

Bear much fruit: so shall ye be My disciples.—Let me beg every reader to consider these words most seriously. Be not content with the thought of gradually doing a little more or better work. In this way it may never come. Take the words, *much fruit,* as the revelation of your heavenly

Vine of what you must be, of what you can be. Accept fully the impossibility, the utter folly of attempting it in your strength. Let the words call you to look anew upon the Vine and undertake to live out its heavenly fullness in you. Let them waken in you once again the faith and the confession: "I am a branch of the true Vine; I can bear much fruit to His glory, and the glory of the Father."

We need not judge others. But we see in God's Word everywhere two classes of disciples. Let there be no hesitation as to where we take our place. Let us ask Him to reveal to us how He asks and claims a life wholly given up to Him, to be as full of His Spirit as He can make us. Let our desire be nothing less than perfect cleansing, unbroken abiding, closest communion, abundant fruitfulness—true branches of the true Vine.

The world is perishing, the church is failing, Christ's cause is suffering, Christ is grieving on account of the lack of wholehearted Christians, bearing much fruit. Though you hardly see what it implies or how it is to come, say to Him that you are His branch to bear much fruit; that you are ready to be His disciple in His own meaning of the word.

*   *   *

My disciples. Blessed Lord, much fruit is the proof that Thou the true Vine hast in me a true branch, a disciple wholly at Thy disposal. Give me, I pray Thee, the childlike consciousness that my fruit is pleasing to Thee, what Thou countest much fruit.

THE WONDERFUL LOVE

*Even as the Father Hath Loved Me, I Also Have
    Loved You.* John 15:9

HERE CHRIST LEAVES the language of parable,
and speaks plainly out of the Father. Much
as the parable could teach, it could not
teach the lesson of love. All that the vine
does for the branch, it does under the compulsion of a law of nature: there is no personal living love to the branch. We are in
danger of looking to Christ as a Saviour
and a supplier of every need, appointed by
God, accepted and trusted by us, without
any sense of the intensity of personal af-
fection in which Christ embraces us, and
our life alone can find its true happiness.
Christ seeks to point us to this.

And how does He do so? He leads us
once again to Himself, to show us how iden-

tical His own life is with ours. Even as the Father loved Him, He loves us. His life as vine dependent on the Father was a life in the Father's love; that love was His strength and His joy; in the power of that divine love resting on Him He lived and died. If we are to live like Him, as branches to be truly like our Vine, we must share in this too. *Our life must have its breath and being in a heavenly love as much as His.* What the Father's love was to Him, His love will be to us. If that love made Him the true Vine, His love can make us true branches. "Even as the Father hath loved me, so have I loved you."

Even as the Father hath loved Me. — And how did the Father love Him? The infinite desire and delight of God to communicate to the Son all He had Himself, to take the Son into the most complete equality with Himself, to live in the Son and have the Son live in Him—this was the love of God to Christ. It is a mystery of glory of which we can form no conception, we can only bow and worship as we try to think of it. And with such a love, with this very same love, Christ longs in an infinite desire and delight to communicate to us all He is and has, to make us partakers of His own nature and blessedness, to live in us and have us live in Himself.

And now, if Christ loves us with such an intense, such an infinite divine love, what is it that hinders it triumphing over every obstacle and getting full possession of us? The answer is simple. Even as the love of the Father to Christ, so His love to us is a divine mystery, too high for us to comprehend or attain to by any effort of our own. It is only the Holy Spirit who can shed abroad and reveal in its all-conquering power without intermission this wonderful love of God in Christ. It is the vine itself that must give the branch its growth and fruit by sending up its sap. It is Christ Himself must by His Holy Spirit dwell in the heart; then shall we know and have in us the love that passeth knowledge.

As the Father loved Me, so have I loved you. —Shall we not draw near to the personal living Christ, and trust Him, and yield all to Him, that He may love this love into us? Just as He knew and rejoiced every hour—the Father loveth Me—we too may live in the unceasing consciousness—as the Father loved Him, so He loves me.

* * *

As the Father loved Me, so have I loved you. Dear Lord, I am only beginning to apprehend how exactly the life of the Vine is to be that of the branch too. Thou art the Vine, because the Father loved Thee, and poured His love

79

through Thee. And so Thou lovest me, and my life as branch is to be like Thine, a receiving and a giving out of heavenly love.

ABIDE IN MY LOVE

---

*Even as the Father Hath Loved Me, I Also Have
Loved You: Abide Ye in My Love.* John 15:9

ABIDE IN MY LOVE.—We speak of a man's
home as his abode. Our abode, the home of
our soul, is to be the love of Christ. We are
to live our life there, to be at home there all
the day: this is what Christ means our life
to be, and really can make it. Our continuous abiding in the Vine is to be an
abiding in His love.

You have probably heard or read of
what is called the higher or the deeper life,
of the richer or the fuller life, of the life
abundant. And you possibly know that
some have told of a wonderful change, by
which their life of continual failure and
stumbling had been changed into a very
blessed experience of being kept and

strengthened and made exceeding glad. If you asked them how it was this great blessing came to them, many would tell you it was simply this, that they were led to believe that this abiding in Christ's love was meant to be a reality, and that they were made willing to give up everything for it, and then enabled to trust Christ to make it true to them.

The love of the Father to the Son is not a sentiment—it is a divine life, an infinite energy, an irresistible power. It carried Christ through life and death and the grave. The Father loved Him and dwelt in Him, and did all for Him. So the love of Christ to us too is an infinite living power that will work in us all He delights to give us. The feebleness of our Christian life is that we do not take time to believe that this divine love does really delight in us, and will possess and work all in us. We do not take time to look at the Vine bearing the branch so entirely, working all in it so completely. We strive to do for ourselves what Christ alone can, what Christ, oh, so lovingly, longs to do for us.

And this now is the secret of the change we spoke of, and the beginning of a new life, when the soul sees this infinite love willing to do all, and gives itself up to it. "Abide ye in my love." To believe that, it is possible so to live moment by moment; to believe that everything that makes it difficult or impossible will be overcome by Christ Himself; to believe that Love really means an infinite longing to give itself wholly to us and never leave us; and in this faith to cast ourselves on Christ to work it in us; this is the secret of the true Christian life.

And how to come to this faith? Turn away from the visible if you would see and possess the invisible. Take more time with Jesus, gazing on Him as the heavenly Vine, living in the love of the Father, wanting you to live in His love. Turn away from yourself and your efforts and your faith, if you would have the heart filled with Him and the certainty of His love. Abiding means going out from everything else, to occupy one place and stay there. Come away from all else, and set your heart on Jesus, and His love, that love will waken your faith and strengthen it. Occupy yourself with that love, worship it, wait for it. You may be sure it will reach out to you, and by its power take you up into itself as your abode and your home.

* * *

Abide in My love. Lord Jesus, I see it, it was Thy abiding in Thy Father's love that made Thee the true Vine, with Thy divine fullness of love and blessing for us. Oh, that I may even so, as a branch, abide in Thy love, for its fullness to fill me and overflow on all around.

OBEY AND ABIDE

If Ye Keep My Commandments, Ye Shall Abide in My Love. John 15:10

IN OUR FORMER MEDITATION reference was made to the entrance into a life of rest and strength which has often come through a true insight into the personal love of Christ, and the assurance that love indeed meant that He would keep the soul. In connection with that transition, and the faith that sees and accepts it, the word *surrender* or *consecration* is frequently used. The soul sees that it cannot claim the keeping of this wonderful love unless it yields itself to a life of entire obedience. It sees too that the faith that can trust Christ for keeping from sinning must prove its sincerity by venturing at once to trust Him for strength to obey. In that faith it dares to give up and cut off

85

everything that has hitherto hindered it, and to promise and expect to live a life that is well pleasing to God.

This is the thought we have here now in our Saviour's teaching. After having in the words, "Abide in my love," spoken of a life in His love as a necessity, because it is at once a possibility and an obligation, He states what its one condition is: *If ye keep my commandments, ye shall abide in my love.*" This is surely not meant to close the door to the abode of His love which He had just opened up. Not in the most distant way does it suggest the thought which some are too ready to entertain, that as we cannot keep His commandments, we cannot abide in His love. No; the precept is a promise: "Abide in my love," could not be a precept if it were not a promise. And so the instruction as to the way through this open door points to no unattainable ideal; the love that invites to her blessed abode reaches out the hand, and enables us to keep the commandments. Let us not fear, in the strength of our ascended Lord, to take the vow of obedience, and give ourselves to the keeping of His commandments. Through His will, loved and done, lies the path to His love.

Only let us understand well what it means. It refers to our performance of all

that we know to be God's will. There may
be doubtful things, of which we are not
sure. A sin of ignorance has still the nature
of sin in it. There may be involuntary sins,
which rise up in the flesh, which we cannot
control or overcome. With regard to these
God will deal in due time in the way of searching and humbling, and if we be simple
and faithful, give us larger deliverance
than we dare expect. But all this may be
found in a truly obedient soul. Obedience
has reference to the positive keeping of the
commandments of our Lord, and the performance of His will in everything in which
we know it. This is a possible degree of
grace, and it is the acceptance in Christ's
strength of such obedience as the purpose
of our heart, of which our Saviour speaks
here. Faith in Christ as our Vine, in His
enabling and sanctifying power, fits us for
this obedience of faith, and secures a life of
abiding in His love.

*If ye keep My commandments, ye shall
abide in My love.* —It is the heavenly Vine
unfolding the mystery of the life He gives. It
is to those abiding in Him to whom He
opens up the secret of the full abiding in
His love. *It is the wholehearted surrender
in everything to do His will, that gives access to a life in the abiding enjoyment of His
love.*

* * *

Obey and abide. Gracious Lord, teach me this lesson, that it is only through knowing Thy will one can know Thy heart, and only through *doing that will* one can abide in Thy love. Lord, teach me that as worthless as is the doing in my own strength, so essential and absolutely indispensable is the *doing* of faith in Thy strength, if I would abide in Thy love.

YE, EVEN AS I

If Ye Keep My Commandments, Ye Shall Abide in My Love, Even as I Have Kept My Father's Commandments, and Abide in His Love. John 15:10

WE HAVE HAD occasion more than once to speak of the perfect similarity of the vine and the branch in nature, and therefore in aim. Here Christ speaks no longer in a parable, but tells us plainly of how His own life is the exact model of ours. He had said that it is alone by obedience we can abide in His love. He now tells that this was the way in which He abode in the Father's love. As the Vine, so the branch. His life and strength and joy had been in the love of the Father: it was only by obedience He abode in it. We may find our life and strength and joy in His love all the day, but it is only by an obedience like His we can abide in it. Perfect conformity to the Vine is one of the most precious of the lessons of the branch. It was by obedience Christ as Vine honored the Father as Husbandman; it is by obedience the believer as branch honors Christ as Vine.

Obey and abide.—That was the law of Christ's life as much as it is to be that of ours. He was made like us in all things, that we might be like Him in all things. He opened up a path in which we may walk even as He walked. He took our human nature to teach us how to wear it, and show us how obedience, as it is the first duty of the creature, is the only way to abide in the favor of God and enter into His glory. And now He comes to instruct and encourage us, and asks us to keep His commandments, even as He kept His Father's commandments and abides in His love.

The divine fitness of this connection between obeying and abiding, between God's commandments and His love, is easily seen. God's will is the very center of His divine perfection. As revealed in His commandments, it opens up the way for the creature to grow into the likeness of the Creator. In accepting and doing His will, I rise into fellowship with Him. Therefore it was that the Son, when coming into the world, spoke: "I come to do thy will, O God"! This was the place and this would be the blessedness of the creature. This was what he had lost in the Fall. This was what Christ came to restore. This is what, as the heavenly Vine, He asks of us and imparts to us, that even as He by keeping His Father's commandments abode in His love, we should keep His commandments and abide in His love.

Ye, even as I.—The branch cannot bear fruit except as it has exactly the same life as the Vine. Our life is to be the exact counterpart of Christ's life. It can be, just in such measure as we believe in Him as the Vine, imparting Himself and His life to His branches. "Ye, even as I," the Vine says; one law, one nature, one fruit. Do let us take from our Lord the lesson of obedience as the secret of abiding. Let us confess that simple, implicit, universal obedience has taken too little the place it should have. Christ died for us as enemies, when we were disobedient. He took us up into His love; now that we are in Him, His Word is: "Obey and abide; ye, even as I." Let us give ourselves to a willing and loving obedience. He will keep us abiding in His love.

* * *

Ye, even as I. O my blessed Vine, who makest the branch in everything partaker of Thy life and likeness, in this too I am to be like Thee: as Thy life in the Father's love through obedience, so mine in Thy love! Saviour, help me, that obedience may indeed be the link between Thee and me.

JOY

These things Have I Spoken Unto You, That My Joy May Be in You, and That Your Joy May Be Fulfilled. John 15:11

IF ANY ONE ASKS the question, "How can I be a happy Christian?" our Lord's answer is very simple: "These things," about the Vine and the branches, "I have spoken to you, that My joy may be in you, and that your joy may be fulfilled." "You cannot have My joy without My life. Abide in Me, and let Me abide in you, and My joy will be in you." All healthy life is a thing of joy and beauty; live undividedly the branch life; you will have His joy in full measure.

To many Christians the thought of a life wholly abiding in Christ is one of strain and painful effort. They cannot see that the strain and effort only come as long as we do not yield ourselves unreservedly to the life of Christ in us. The very first words of the parable are not yet opened up to them: "I am the true Vine; I undertake all and provide for all; I ask nothing of the branch but that it yields wholly to Me, and allows Me to do all. *I engage to make and keep the branch all that it ought to be.*" Ought it not to be an infinite and unceasing joy to have the Vine thus work all, and to know that it is none less than the blessed Son of God in His love who is each moment bearing us and maintaining our life?

That My joy may be in you.—We are to have Christ's own joy in us. And what is Christ's own joy? There is no joy like love. There is no joy but love. Christ had just spoken of the Father's love and His own abiding in it, and of His having loved us with that same love. His joy is nothing but the joy of love, of being loved and of loving. It was the joy of receiving His Father's love and abiding in it, and then the joy of passing on that love and pouring it out on sinners. It is this joy He wants us to share: the joy of being loved of the Father and of Him; the joy of in our turn loving and living for those around us. This is just the joy of being truly branches: abiding in His love, and then giving up ourselves in love to bear fruit for others. Let us accept His life, as He gives it in us as the Vine, His joy will be ours: the joy of abiding in His love, the joy of loving like Him, of loving with His love.

And that your joy may be fulfilled. —That it may be complete, that you may be filled with it. How sad that we should so need to be reminded that as God alone is the fountain of all joy, "God our exceeding joy," the only way to be perfectly happy is to have as much of God, as much of His will and fellowship, as possible! Religion is meant to be in everyday life a thing of unspeakable joy. And why do so many complain that it is not so? Because they do not believe that there is no joy like the joy of abiding in Christ and in His love, and being branches through whom He can pour out His love on a dying world.

Oh, that Christ's voice might reach the heart of every young Christian, and persuade him to believe that His joy is the only true joy, that His joy can become ours and truly fill us, and that the sure and simple way of living in it is—only this—to abide as branches in Him our heavenly Vine. Let the truth enter deep into us—as long as our joy is not full, it is a sign that we do not yet know our heavenly Vine aright; every desire for a fuller joy must only urge us to abide more simply and more fully in His love.

* * *

My joy—your joy. In this too it is: as the Vine, so the branch; all the Vine in the branch. Thy joy is our joy—Thy joy in us, and our joy fulfilled. Blessed Lord, fill me with Thy joy—the joy of being loved and blessed with a divine love; the joy of loving and blessing others.

LOVE ONE ANOTHER

This is My Commandment, That Ye Love One Another. John 15:12

GOD IS LOVE. His whole nature and perfection is love, living not for Himself, but to dispense life and blessing. In His love He begat the Son, that He might give all to Him. In His love He brought forth creatures that He might make them partakers of His blessedness.

Christ is the Son of God's love, the bearer, the revealer, the communicator of that love. His life and death were all love. Love is His life, and the life He gives. He only lives to love, to live out His life of love in us, to give Himself in all who will receive Him. The very first thought of the true Vine is love—living only to impart His life to the branches.

The Holy Spirit is the Spirit of love. He cannot impart Christ's life without imparting His love. Salvation is nothing but love conquering and entering into us; we have just as much of salvation as we have of love. Full salvation is perfect love.

No wonder that Christ said: "A new commandment I give unto you"; "This is my commandment"—the one all-inclusive commandment—"that ye love one another." The branch is not only one with the vine, but with all its other branches; they drink one spirit, they form one body, they bear one fruit. Nothing can be more unnatural than that Christians should not love one another, even as Christ loved them. The life they received from their heavenly Vine is nothing but love. This is the one thing He asks above all others. "Hereby shall all men know that ye are my disciples . . . love one another." As the special sort of vine is known by the fruit it bears, the nature of the heavenly Vine is to be judged of by the love His disciples have to one another.

See that you obey this commandment. Let your "obey and abide" be seen in this. Love your brethren as the way to abide in the love of your Lord. Let your vow of obedience begin here. Love one another. Let your intercourse with the Christians in your own family be holy, tender, Christlike love. Let your thoughts of the Christians round you be, before everything, in the spirit of Christ's love. Let your life and conduct be the sacrifice of love—give yourself up to think of their sins or their needs, to intercede for them, to help and to serve them. Be in your church or circle the embodiment of Christ's love. The life Christ lives in you is love; let the life in which you live it out be all love.

But, man, you write as if all this was so natural and simple and easy. Is it at all possible thus to live and thus to love? My answer is: Christ commands it: you must obey. Christ means it: you must obey, or you cannot abide in His love.

But I have tried and failed. I see no prospect of living like Christ. Ah! that is because you have failed to take in the first word of the parable—"I am the true Vine: I give all you need as a branch, I give all I myself have." I pray you, let the sense of past failure and present feebleness drive you to the Vine. He is all love. He loves to give. He gives love. He will teach you to love, even as He loved.

* * *

Love one another. Dear Lord Jesus, Thou art all love; the life Thou gavest us is love; Thy new commandment, and Thy badge of discipleship is, "Love one another." I accept the charge: with the love with which Thou lovest me, and I love Thee, I will love my brethren.

EVEN AS I HAVE LOVED YOU

This is My Commandment, That Ye Love One Another, Even as I Have Loved You. John 15:12

THIS IS THE SECOND TIME our Lord uses the expression—*Even as I.* The first time it was of His relation to the Father, keeping His commandments, and abiding in His love. Even so we are to keep Christ's commandments, and abide in His love. The second time He speaks of His relation to us as the rule of our love to our brethren: "Love one another, as I have loved you." In each case His disposition and conduct is to be the law for ours. It is again the truth we have more than once insisted on—perfect likeness between the Vine and the branch.

Even as I.—But is it not a vain thing to imagine that we can keep His commandments, and love the brethren, even as He kept His Father's, and as He loved us? And must not the attempt end in failure and discouragement? Undoubtedly, if we seek to carry out the injunction in our strength, or without a full apprehension of the truth of the Vine and its branches. But if we understand that the "even as I" is just the one great lesson of the parable, the one continual language of the Vine to the branch, we shall see that it is not the question of what we feel able to accomplish, but of what Christ is able to work in us. These high and holy commands—"Obey, even as I! Love, even as I"—are just meant to bring us to the consciousness of our impotence, and through that to waken us to the need and the beauty and the sufficiency of what is provided for us in the Vine. We shall begin to hear the Vine speaking every moment to the branch: "Even as I. Even as I: My life is your life; you have a share in all My fullness; the Spirit in you, and the fruit that comes from you, is all just the same as in Me. Be not afraid, but let your faith grasp each 'Even as I' as the divine assurance that because I live in you, you may and can live like Me."

But why, if this really be the meaning of the parable, if this really be the life a branch may live, why do so few realize it?

Because they do not know the heavenly mystery of the Vine. They know much of the parable and its beautiful lessons. But the hidden spiritual mystery of the Vine in His divine omnipotence and nearness, bearing and supplying them all the day—this they do not know, because they have not waited on God's Spirit to reveal it to them.

Love one another, even as I have loved you.—"Ye, even as I." How are we to begin if we are really to learn the mystery? With the confession that we need to be brought to an entirely new mode of life, because we have never yet known Christ as the Vine in the completeness of His quickening and transforming power. With the surrender to be cleansed from all that is of self, and detached from all that is in the world, to live only and wholly as Christ lived for the glory of the Father. And then with the faith that this "even as I" is indeed what Christ is ready to make true, the Vine will maintain that very life in the branch wholly dependent upon Him.

* * *

Even as I. Ever again it is, my blessed Lord, as the Vine, so the branch—one life, one spirit, one obedience, one joy, one love.

Lord Jesus, *in the faith that Thou art my Vine, and that I am Thy branch,* I accept Thy command as a promise, and take Thy "even as

I" as the simple revelation of what Thou dost work in me. Yea, Lord, as Thou hast loved, I will love.

CHRIST'S FRIENDSHIP: ITS ORIGIN

Greater Love Hath No Man Than This, That a Man Lay Down His Life for His Friends.
John 15:13

IN THE THREE following verses our Lord speaks of His relation to His disciples under a new aspect—that of friendship. He points us to the love in which it on His side has its origin (v. 13); to the obedience on our part by which it is maintained (v. 14); and then to the holy intimacy to which it leads (v. 15).

Our relation to Christ is one of love. In speaking of this previously, He showed us what His love was in its heavenly glory; the same love with which the Father had loved Him. Here we have it in its earthly manifestation—laying down His life for us.

"Greater love hath no man than this, that a man lay down his life for his friends." Christ does indeed long to have us know that the secret root and strength of all He is and does for us as the Vine is love. As we learn to believe this, we shall feel that here is something which we not only need to think and know about, but a living power, a divine life which we need to receive within us. Christ and His love are inseparable; they are identical. God is love, and Christ is love. God and Christ and the divine love can only be known *by having them*, by their life and power working within us. "This is eternal *life*, that they *know* thee"; there is no knowing God but by having the life; the life working in us *alone gives the knowledge.* And even so the love; if we would know it, we must drink of its living stream, we must have it shed forth by the Holy Spirit in us.

"Greater love hath no man than this, that a man give his life for his friends." The life is the most precious thing a man has; the life is all he is; the life is himself. This is the highest measure of love: when a man gives his life, he holds nothing back, he gives all he has and is. It is this our Lord Jesus wants to make clear to us concerning His mystery of the Vine; with all He has He has placed Himself at our disposal. He wants us to count Him our very own; He wants to be wholly our possession, that we may be wholly His possession. He gave His life for us in death not merely as a passing act, that when accomplished was done with; no, but as a making Himself ours for eternity. Life for life; He gave His life for us to possess that we might give our life for Him to possess. This is what is taught by the parable of the Vine and the branch, in their wonderful indentification, in their perfect union.

It is as we know something of this, not by reason or imagination, but deep down in the heart and life, that we shall begin to see what ought to be our life as branches of the heavenly Vine. He gave Himself to death; He lost Himself, that we might find life in Him. This is the true Vine, who only lives to live in us. This is the beginning and the root of that holy friendship to which Christ invites us.

Great is the mystery of godliness! Let us confess our ignorance and unbelief. Let us cease from our own understanding and our own efforts to master it. Let us wait for the Holy Spirit who dwells within us to reveal it. Let us trust His infinite love, which gave its life for us, to take possession and rejoice in making us wholly its own.

* * *

His life for His friends. How wonderful the lessons of the Vine, giving its very life to its branches! And Jesus gave His life for His friends. And that love gives itself to them and in them. My heavenly Vine, oh, teach me how wholly Thou longest to live in me!

CHRIST'S FRIENDSHIP: ITS EVIDENCE

Ye Are My Friends, if Ye Do the Things Which I Command You. John 15:14

OUR LORD HAS SAID what He gave as proof of His friendship: He gave His life for us. He now tells us what our part is to be—to do the things which He commands. He gave His life to secure a place for His love in our hearts to rule us; the response His love calls us to, and empowers us for, is that we do what He commands us. As we know the dying love, we shall joyfully obey its commands. As we obey the commands, we shall know the love more fully. Christ had already said: "If ye keep my commandments, ye shall abide in my love." He counts it needful to repeat the truth again: the one proof of our faith in His love, the one way to abide in it, the one mark of being true branches is—to do the things which He commands us. He began with absolute surrender of His life for us. He can ask nothing less from us. This alone is a life in His friendship.

This truth, of the imperative necessity of obedience, doing all that Christ commands us, has not the place in our Christian teaching and living that Christ meant it to have. We have given a far higher place to privilege than to duty. We have not considered implicit obedience as a condition of true discipleship. The secret thought that it is impossible to do the things He commands us, and that therefore it cannot be expected of us, and a subtle and unconscious feeling that sinning is a necessity have frequently robbed both precepts and promises of their power. The whole relation to Christ has become clouded and lowered, the waiting on His teaching, the power to hear and obey His voice, and through obedience to enjoy His love and friendship, have been enfeebled by the terrible mistake. Do let us try to return to the true position, take Christ's words as most literally true, and make nothing less the law of our life: "Ye are my friends, *if ye do* the things that I command you." Surely our Lord asks nothing less than that we heartily and truthfully say: "Yea, Lord, what Thou dost command, that will I do."

These commands are to be done as a proof of friendship. The power to do them rests entirely in the personal relationship to Jesus. For a friend I could do what I would not for another. The friendship of Jesus is so heavenly and wonderful, it comes to us so as the power of a divine love entering in and taking possession, the unbroken fellowship with Himself is so essential to it, that it implies and imparts a joy and a love which make the obedience a delight. The liberty to claim the friendship of Jesus, the power to enjoy it, the grace to prove it in all its blessedness—all come as we do the things He commands us.

Is not the one thing needful for us that we ask our Lord to reveal Himself to us in the dying love in which He proved Himself our friend, and then listen as He says to us: "Ye are My friends." As we see what our Friend has done for us, and what an unspeakable blessedness it is to have Him call us friends, the doing His commands will become the natural fruit of our life in His love. We shall not fear to say: "Yea, Lord, we are Thy friends, and do what Thou dost command us."

* * *

If ye do. Yes, it is in *doing* that we are blessed, that we abide in His love, that we enjoy His friendship. "If ye do what I command you!" O my Lord, let Thy holy friendship lead me into the love of all Thy commands, and let the doing of Thy commands lead me ever deeper into Thy friendship.

CHRIST'S FRIENDSHIP:
ITS INTIMACY

No Longer Do I Call You Servants; for the Servant Knoweth Not What His Lord Doeth: But I Have Called You Friends; for All Things That I Heard From My Father, I Have Made Known Unto You. John 15:15

THE HIGHEST PROOF of true friendship, and one great source of its blessedness, is the intimacy that holds nothing back, and admits the friend to share our inmost secrets. It is a blessed thing to be Christ's servant; His redeemed ones delight to call themselves His slaves. Christ had often spoken of the disciples as His servants. In His great love our Lord now says: "No longer do I call you servants"; with the coming of the Holy Spirit a new era was to be inaugurated. "The servant knoweth not

113

what his Lord doeth"—he has to obey without being consulted or admitted into the secret of all his master's plans. "*But, I have called you friends, for all things I heard from my Father I have made known unto you.*" Christ's friends share with Him in all the secrets the Father has entrusted to Him.

Let us think what this means. When Christ spoke of keeping His Father's commandments, He did not mean merely what was written in Holy Scripture, but those special commandments which were communicated to Him day by day, and from hour to hour. It was of these He said: "The Father loveth the Son, and showeth him all things that he doeth, and he will show him greater things." All that Christ did was God's working. God showed it to Christ, so that He carried out the Father's will and purpose, not, as man often does, blindly and unintelligently, but with full understanding and approval. As one who stood in God's counsel, He knew God's plan.

And this now is the blessedness of being Christ's friends, that we do not, as servants, do His will without much spiritual insight into its meaning and aim, but are admitted, as an inner circle, into some knowledge of God's more secret thoughts.

From the Day of Pentecost on, by the Holy Spirit, Christ was to lead His disciples into the spiritual apprehension of the mysteries of the kingdom, of which He had hitherto spoken only by parables.

Friendship delights in fellowship. Friends hold council. Friends dare trust to each other what they would not for anything have others know. What is it that gives a Christian access to this holy intimacy with Jesus? That gives him the spiritual capacity for receiving the communications Christ has to make of what the Father has shown Him? "Ye are my friends *if ye do what I command you.*" It is loving obedience that purifies the soul. That refers not only to the commandments of the Word, but to that blessed application of the Word to our daily life, which none but our Lord Himself can give. But as these are waited for in dependence and humility, and faithfully obeyed, the soul becomes fitted for ever-closer fellowship, and the daily life may become a continual experience: "I have called you friends; for all things I have heard from my Father, I have made known unto you."

* * *

I have called you friends. What an unspeakable honor! What a heavenly privilege! O Saviour, speak the word with power into my

115

soul: "I have called you My friend, whom I love, whom I trust, to whom I make known all that passes between my Father and Me."

ELECTION

Ye Did Not Choose Me, But I Chose You, and Appointed You That Ye Should Go and Bear Fruit. John 15:16

THE BRANCH does not choose the vine, or decide on which vine it will grow. The vine brings forth the branch, as and where it will. Even so Christ says: "Ye did not choose me, but I chose you." But some will say is not just this the difference between the branch in the natural and in the spiritual world, that man has a will and a power of choosing, and that it is in virtue of his having decided to accept Christ, his having chosen Him as Lord, that he is now a branch? This is undoubtedly true. And yet it is only half a truth. The lesson of the Vine, and the teaching of our Lord, points to the other half, the deeper, the divine side of our being in Christ. If He had not chosen us, we had never chosen Him. Our choosing Him was the result of His choosing us, and taking hold of us. In the very nature of things, it is His prerogative as Vine to choose and create His own branch. We owe all we are to "the election of grace." If we want to know Christ as the true Vine, the sole origin and strength of the branch life, and ourselves as branches in our absolute, most blessed, and most secure dependence upon Him, let us drink deep of this blessed truth: "Ye did not choose me, but I chose you."

And with what view does Christ say this? That they may know what the object is for which He chose them, and find, in their faith in His election, the certainty of fulfilling their destiny. Throughout Scripture this is the great object of the teaching of election. "Predestinated to be conformed to the image of his son" (to be branches in the image and likeness of the Vine). "Chosen that we should be holy." "Chosen to salvation, through sanctification of the Spirit." "Elect in sanctification of the Spirit unto obedience." Some have abused the doctrine of election, and others, for fear of its abuse, have rejected it, because they have overlooked this teaching. They have occupied themselves with its hidden origin in eternity, with the inscrutable mysteries of the counsels of God, instead of accepting the revelation of its purpose in time, and the blessings it brings into our Christian life.

Just think what these blessings are. In our verse Christ reveals His twofold purpose in choosing us to be His branches: that we may bear fruit on earth, and have power in prayer in Heaven. What confidence the thought that He has chosen us for this gives, that He will not fail to fit us for carrying out His purpose! What assurance that we can bear fruit that will abide, and can pray so as to obtain! What a continual call to the deepest humility and praise, to the most entire dependence and expectancy! He would not choose us for what we are not fit for, or what He could not fit us for. He has chosen us; this is the pledge, He will do all in us.

Let us listen in silence of soul to our holy Vine speaking to each of us: "You did not choose Me!" And let us say, "Yes, Lord, but I chose You! Amen, Lord!" Ask Him to show what this means. In Him, the true Vine, your life as branch has its divine origin, its eternal security, and the power to fulfill His purpose. From Him to whose will of love you owe all, you may expect all. In Him, His purpose, and His power, and His faithfulness, in His love let me abide.

* * *

I chose you. Lord, teach me what this means—that Thou hast set Thy heart on me, and chosen me to bear fruit that will abide, and to pray prayer that will prevail. In this Thine eternal purpose my soul would rest itself and say: "What He chose me for I *will* be, I *can* be, I *shall* be."

ABIDING FRUIT

I Chose You, and Appointed You, That Ye Should Go and Bear Fruit, and That Your Fruit Should Abide. John 15:16

THERE ARE SOME FRUITS that will not keep. One sort of pears or apples must be used at once; another sort can be kept over till next year. So there is in Christian work some fruit that does not last. There may be much that pleases and edifies, and yet there is no permanent impression made on the power of the world or the state of the Church. On the other hand, there is work that leaves its mark for generations or for eternity. In it the power of God makes itself lastingly felt. It is the fruit of which Paul speaks when he describes the two styles of ministry: "My preaching was not in persuasive words of wisdom, but in demonstration of the Spirit and of power; that your faith should not stand in the wisdom of men, but in the power of God." The more of man with his wisdom and power, the less of stability; the more of God's Spirit, the more of a faith standing in God's power.

Fruit reveals the nature of the tree from which it comes. What is the secret of bearing fruit that abides? The answer is simple. It is as our life abides in Christ, as we abide in Him, that the fruit we bear will abide. The more we allow all that is of human will and effort to be cut down short and cleansed away by the divine Husbandman, the more intensely our being withdraws itself from the outward that God may work in us by His Spirit; that is, the more wholly we abide in Christ, the more will our fruit abide.

What a blessed thought! He chose you, and appointed you to bear fruit, *and that your fruit should abide.* He never meant one of His branches to bring forth fruit that should not abide. The deeper I enter into the purpose of this His electing grace, the surer my confidence will become that I can bring forth fruit to eternal life, for myself and others. The deeper I enter into this purpose of His electing love, the more I will realize what the link is between the purpose from eternity, and the fruit to eternity: the abiding in Him. The purpose is His, He will carry it out; the fruit is His, He will bring it forth; the abiding is His, He will maintain it.

Let everyone who professes to be a Christian worker, pause. Ask whether you are leaving your mark for eternity on those around you. It is not your preaching or teaching, your strength of will or power to influence, that will secure this. *All depends on having your life full of God and His power.* And that again depends upon your living the truly branchlike life of abiding —very close and unbroken fellowship with Christ. It is the branch, that abides in Him, that brings forth much fruit, fruit that will abide.

Blessed Lord, reveal to my soul, I pray Thee, that Thou hast chosen me to bear much fruit. Let this be my confidence, that Thy purpose can be realized—Thou didst choose me. Let this be my power to forsake everything and give myself to Thee. Thou wilt Thyself perfect what Thou hast begun. Draw me so to dwell in the love and the certainty of that eternal purpose, that the power of eternity may possess me, and the fruit I bear may abide.

* * *

That ye may bear fruit. O my heavenly Vine, it is beginning to dawn upon my soul that fruit, more fruit—much fruit—abiding fruit is the one thing Thou hast to give me, and the one thing as branch I have to give Thee! Here I am. Blessed Lord, work out Thy purpose in me; let me bear much fruit, abiding fruit, to Thy glory.

PREVAILING PRAYER

I Appointed You That Ye Should Go and Bear Fruit, and That Your Fruit Should Abide: That Whatsoever Ye Shall Ask of the Father in My Name, He May Give It You. John 15:16

IN THE FIRST VERSE of our parable, Christ revealed Himself as the true Vine, and the Father as the Husbandman, and asked for Himself and the Father a place in the heart. Here, in the closing verse, He sums up all His teaching concerning Himself and the Father in the twofold purpose for which He had chosen them. With reference to Himself, the Vine, the purpose was, that they should bear fruit. With reference to the Father, it was, that whatsoever they should ask in His name, should be done of the Father in Heaven. As fruit is the great proof of the true relation to Christ, so prayer is of our relation to the Father. A fruitful abiding in the Son, and prevailing prayer to the Father, are the two great factors in the true Christian life.

That whatsoever ye shall ask of the Father in my name, he may give it you.—These are the closing words of the parable of the Vine. The whole mystery of the Vine and its branches leads up to the other mystery—that *whatsoever we ask in His name the Father gives!* See here the reason of the lack of prayer, and of the lack of power in prayer. It is because we so little live the true branch life, because we so little lose ourselves in the Vine, abiding in Him entirely, that we feel so little constrained to much prayer, so little confident that we shall be heard, and so do not know how to use His name as the key to God's storehouse. The Vine planted on earth has reached up into Heaven; it is only the soul wholly and intensely abiding in it that can reach into Heaven with power to prevail much. Our faith in the teaching and the truth of the parable, in the truth and the life of the Vine, must prove itself by power in prayer. The life of abiding and obedience, of love and joy, of cleansing and fruit-bearing, will surely lead to the power of prevailing prayer.

Whatsoever ye shall ask.—The promise

was given to disciples who were ready to give themselves, in the likeness of the true Vine, for their fellow men. This promise was all their provision for their work; they took it literally, they believed it, they used it, and they found it true. Let us give ourselves, as branches of the true Vine, and in His likeness, to the work of saving men, of bringing forth fruit to the glory of God, and we shall find a new urgency and power to pray and to claim the "whatsoever ye ask." We shall waken to our wonderful responsibility of having in such a promise the keys to the King's storehouses given us, and we shall not rest till we have received bread and blessing for the perishing.

"I chose you, that ye may bring forth fruit, and that your fruit may abide; that whatsoever ye shall ask of the Father in my name, he may give it to you." Beloved disciple, seek above everything to be a man of prayer. Here is the highest exercise of your privilege as a branch of the Vine; here is the full proof of your being renewed in the image of God and His Son; here is your power to show how you, like Christ, live not for yourself, but for others; here you enter Heaven to receive gifts for men; here your abiding in Christ has led to His abiding in you, to use you as the channel and instrument of His grace. The power to bear fruit for men has been crowned by power to prevail with God.

"I am the vine, my Father is the Husbandman." Christ's work in you is to bring you so to the Father that His Word may be fulfilled in you: "At that day ye shall ask in my name; and I say not that I will pray the Father for you; for the Father himself loveth you." The power of direct access to the Father for men, the liberty of intercession claiming and receiving blessing for them in faith, is the highest exercise of our union with Christ. Let all who would truly and fully be branches give themselves to the work of intercession. It is the one great work of Christ the Vine in Heaven, the source of power for all His work. Make it your one great work as branch: it will be the power of all your work.

* * *

In My name. Yes, Lord, in Thy name, the new name Thou hast given Thyself here, the true Vine. As a branch, abiding in Thee in entire devotion, in full dependence, in perfect conformity, in abiding fruitfulness, I come to the Father, in Thee, and He will give what I ask. Oh, let my life be one of unceasing and prevailing intercession!